First published in the United States, Great Britain, Canada,
Australia, and New Zealand in 1994 by The Jane Goodall Institute.
Reissued in 1998 by North-South Books,
an imprint of Nord-Süd Verlag AG, Gossau Zürich, Switzerland.

Goodall, Jane.
With love : ten heartwarming stories of chimpanzees in the wild /
by Jane Goodall : illustrated by Alan Marks.
Summary : A collection of stories based on the author's experiences with chimpanzees
in Gombe Stream National Park in Tanzania over a period of almost forty years.
1. Chimpanzees—Tanzania—Gombe Stream National Park—Juvenile literature.
[1. Chimpanzees—Habits and behavior.] I. Marks, Alan. II. Title.
QL737.P96G588 1998
599.885—dc21 97-49948

A CIP catalogue record for this book is available from The British Library.
ISBN 1-55858-911-2 (trade binding)
3 5 7 9 TB 10 8 6 4 2
ISBN 1-55858-912-0 (library binding)
3 5 7 9 LB 10 8 6 4 2
Printed in Belgium

For more information about our books, and the authors and artists
who create them, visit our web site: http://www.northsouth.com

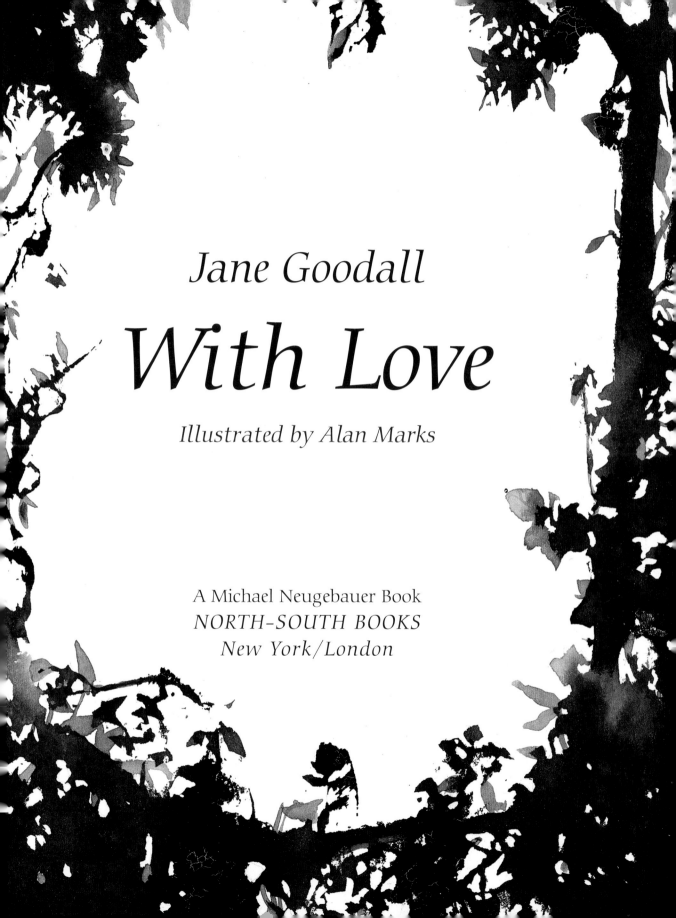

Jane Goodall

With Love

Illustrated by Alan Marks

A Michael Neugebauer Book
NORTH-SOUTH BOOKS
New York/London

In 1960 almost nothing was known about the way chimpanzees live in the wild. That was when I went to Gombe National Park, in Tanzania, to see what I could find out. Every morning I climbed up into the forested mountains before it was light, and stayed up there until dusk. The chimpanzees were terrified of the peculiar white ape who had suddenly appeared in their world, and for months I could watch them only at a distance, through binoculars. If I tried to get too close, they fled. Gradually, though, some of them began to lose their fear.

One evening when I got back to camp, Dominic, my Tanzanian cook, told me that a large male chimpanzee had arrived that morning to feast on the ripe fruits of an oilnut palm growing by my tent. When he left, he had snatched some bananas from my table.

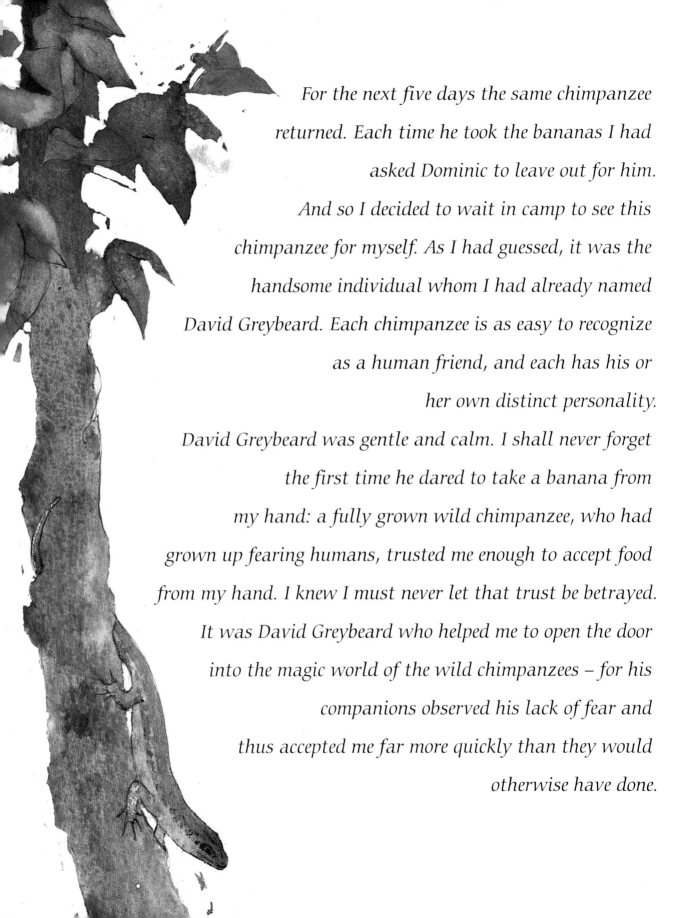

For the next five days the same chimpanzee returned. Each time he took the bananas I had asked Dominic to leave out for him. And so I decided to wait in camp to see this chimpanzee for myself. As I had guessed, it was the handsome individual whom I had already named David Greybeard. Each chimpanzee is as easy to recognize as a human friend, and each has his or her own distinct personality.

David Greybeard was gentle and calm. I shall never forget the first time he dared to take a banana from my hand: a fully grown wild chimpanzee, who had grown up fearing humans, trusted me enough to accept food from my hand. I knew I must never let that trust be betrayed. It was David Greybeard who helped me to open the door into the magic world of the wild chimpanzees – for his companions observed his lack of fear and thus accepted me far more quickly than they would otherwise have done.

David and the others have taught me much. Chimpanzees can, like humans, be very aggressive – even brutal – at times. But they can be so gentle, affectionate, and caring towards each other, too.

It is not only we humans who are capable of love, compassion, and altruism, and the stories recounted here – based on my experiences with chimpanzees over a period of almost forty years – demonstrate this capacity for love.

MEL AND SPINDLE

When Mel was just over three years old, his mother died during an epidemic of pneumonia that claimed the lives of seven other chimpanzees as well. In the wild, orphans are typically adopted and cared for by their elder sisters or brothers – but Mel was alone in the world. And anyway, like all three-year-olds, he was still drinking a good deal of milk – we all thought he would die. It wasn't even as though he was a robust infant. He was sickly and looked frail.

For the first couple of weeks Mel was a pathetic figure. He followed different chimpanzees, begging food from them, occasionally riding on their backs. They were, for the most part, tolerant of him – but he had no special friend, no individual on whom he could rely absolutely for comfort and protection.

And then the miracle happened. Mel was adopted by Spindle, a twelve-year-old adolescent male. Spindle was not closely related to Mel. Indeed, he had never even spent much time with the infant before. Yet now he waited for the orphan during travel, he allowed him to ride on his back or even, if it was raining or if Mel was frightened, to cling to his belly. Spindle always let the infant creep into his nest at night and, in response to Mel's begging gestures, often shared his food. And Spindle would run to defend or rescue his small charge if need arose.

Why did Spindle adopt Mel? We shall never know for sure. Was it,

perhaps, in some way connected with the fact that Spindle's mother, ancient Sprout, died at the same time as Mel's? Of course, a twelve-year-old male does not spend all that much time with his mother – he is off with the adult males, learning about hunting and protecting the territory, and about females. But even so, if his mother is still alive he often returns to her for a while if the going gets tough. In her familiar presence he finds reassurance and comfort. Is it possible that Sprout's death left an empty space in Spindle's heart, a space that was, to some extent, filled by his close contact with a small dependent infant?

Whatever the reason, Spindle saved Mel's life.

THE PIG HUNT

Chimpanzees enjoy eating fresh meat, and they occasionally hunt young bushpigs. This is sometimes dangerous, for wild pigs, as everyone knows, can be very fierce. One day a group of chimpanzees came across some adult pigs with young. The chimpanzees, bristling with excitement, began to hunt. They crashed about in the under-growth, making a lot of commotion, so that the pigs were confused and the hunters had more opportunity to seize a piglet. But even so, each time they tried, they were charged furiously by an adult pig.

Suddenly nine-year-old Freud began to scream in terror and pain. He was young to take part in a pig hunt and his lack of experience had landed him in trouble. He had managed to catch a piglet but he had not been quick enough to climb out of danger. One of the sows, desperately trying to protect her young, had charged Freud and bitten into his rump. There was the sound of tooth on bone.

The piglet escaped and ran off, unharmed.

Freud, screaming louder still, struggled to escape also, but the sow refused to let go. Suddenly a large chimpanzee burst from the undergrowth, charging directly towards Freud and his captor. It was Gigi, large and childless, the Amazon of her community. The sow turned quickly to face this new challenge, and Freud, seizing his opportunity, painfully dragged himself up a tree.

Gigi herself only just escaped, leaping into some low branches with her foot only a few inches from the pig's powerful jaws.

Freud was badly hurt and bled heavily, and it was some weeks before he could walk without limping. Gigi had, without doubt, saved his life.

POM RESCUES HER INFANT BROTHER

One day, eight-year-old Pom was leading her family along a forest trail. Behind her tottered her three-year-old brother, Prof. Their mother, Passion, plodded some distance in the rear.

Suddenly Pom paused, staring at the ground ahead. There, coiled up in the thick undergrowth, was a big snake.

Pom uttered a small call of alarm and, with her hair bristling in fear, quickly climbed a nearby tree.

Prof, however, continued along the trail.

Perhaps he had not heard
Pom's call, or had not under–
stood what it meant. And
Passion was not close enough
to know what was happening.
And so, with Pom watching
from the branches above, Prof
moved ever closer to the
snake. Eventually, when he
was but a few yards (metres)
from it, Pom could bear it no
longer. With her hair bristling
even more, and a big grin of
fear on her face, she leapt to
the ground, gathered her little
brother into her arms, and
carried him back into the tree.
They were safe, and gradually
Pom's hair sleeked and the
grin left her face.
By the time Passion arrived,
the snake had glided away
into the undergrowth.

PROF AND PAX

It was the rainy season, cold and wet. Not surprising that little Pax, just two years old, had a bad head cold.

His nose was stuffed up so that he breathed through his mouth, and he was listless, keeping close to his mother, Passion.

Presently his older brother, Prof, who was seven years old at this time, came over to enjoy a session of social grooming with Passion. Mostly it was she who groomed him, as is the way with mothers and sons. For a while Prof groomed young Pax, who was sitting, breathing noisily, beside them. Then he gave himself up to the sooth-ing pleasure of his mother's gently grooming fingers.

Suddenly Pax was convulsed with a great sneeze. Prof, startled by the explosive sound, turned to look at his small brother. That sneeze had certainly cleared the stuffed-up nose – Pax was a disgusting sight at that moment. Better not to describe it! Prof stared for a moment and then reached out and picked a large handful of leaves. Very gently, very carefully, he wiped the snot from his brother's small face, peered briefly at the soiled leaves, then threw them away and again began grooming the infant. Passion, who had ignored the sneeze, continued to pay attention to her elder son.

Pax, his congestion at least temporarily relieved, and lulled by the rhythmic movements of grooming fingers, fell asleep.

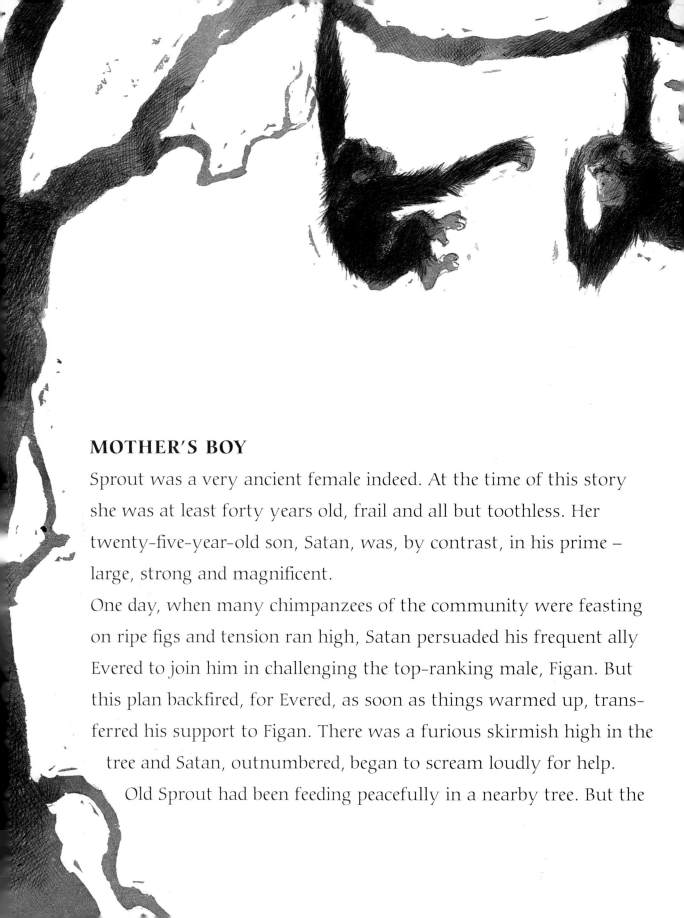

MOTHER'S BOY

Sprout was a very ancient female indeed. At the time of this story she was at least forty years old, frail and all but toothless. Her twenty-five-year-old son, Satan, was, by contrast, in his prime – large, strong and magnificent.

One day, when many chimpanzees of the community were feasting on ripe figs and tension ran high, Satan persuaded his frequent ally Evered to join him in challenging the top-ranking male, Figan. But this plan backfired, for Evered, as soon as things warmed up, transferred his support to Figan. There was a furious skirmish high in the tree and Satan, outnumbered, began to scream loudly for help.

Old Sprout had been feeding peacefully in a nearby tree. But the

moment she heard her son's frenzied calling, she raced to his aid. She leapt from branch to branch and, on arriving at the scene of the battle, hurled herself into the fray. Evered, perhaps irritated by the puny blows of this ancient and frail female, turned and began to hit her – and Satan quickly seized the opportunity to pull away from Figan and escape to the ground.

Now it was Sprout who screamed for help. It would be nice to relate that Satan bravely returned to assist his mother. But no such thing happened! Never mind – she was only cuffed a few times and then she too escaped. Soon all was peaceful and the chim-panzees began to feed again. Satan fed close to his old mother.

FLO AND FLINT

Flo was a wonderful mother, patient, tolerant, affectionate, and playful. She gave her infants the opportunity to explore, yet she watched carefully, and at the slightest sign of real or imagined danger she would hasten to rescue them. In this way she successfully raised three offspring: Faben, Figan, and Fifi. Yet she failed both of her last youngsters.

When Flint was born, Flo already looked old. It was obvious that Faben had not been her first child – before conceiving him, she must have given birth at least twice to offspring who had either died or, if they were females, perhaps emigrated to nearby communities. For it is the females who sometimes disperse in chimpanzee society, thus preventing too much inbreeding. Be that as it may, at the time of Flint's birth Flo's teeth were already worn and her hair was thinning and brown with age. Despite this, Flo remained an aggressive and high-ranking female for the first couple of years of Flint's life. Things began to go wrong when Flint was four years old and Flo started the long process of weaning. The trouble was that Flint had become the chimpanzee equivalent of a "spoiled brat." Not only had he had the benefit of a dominant mother, always ready to protect and support him, but one or other of his elder brothers, or his sister, had usually been around, more than ready to help their young brother should he need them. Thus Flint became thoroughly used to

getting his own way. And when Flo tried to prevent him from suckling, or riding on her back, he resented it bitterly. He threw violent
tantrums. He even hit and bit his mother sometimes. Despite this,
Flo persisted in her efforts.

Things got even worse when, despite the fact that Flint was still
nursing, Flo became pregnant again. She needed all her failing
strength to nurture the life growing within her:
she had less and less energy to cope
with her obstreperous child.

Indeed, had her milk supply not dried up, Flint would have been suckling still when the next baby was born – a female whom we named Flame.

Flint became even more distressed – for now he had to share Flo's attention. He still tried to suckle, but despite his most violent tantrums, this was the one thing that Flo was firm about. However, she gave in when he insisted on riding on her back, and when he pushed into the night nest in the evening. And she acquiesced when he bothered her, endlessly, for social grooming. The burden on Flo grew even as Flame grew larger and Flint was still riding her back while Flame clung on below.

When Flame was six months old, she died. It happened when Flo herself was very, very sick, probably suffering from pneumonia. She lacked the strength to climb into the trees, and lay on the ground, often in the rain. When we found her, Flame had disappeared and we never knew what happened. Probably she died of the same disease, and bushpigs took away her little body.

Flo, to our amazement, recovered. And now, with Flame out of the way, Flint regained his former joie de vivre. But despite his loss of depression, he remained abnormally dependent on his old mother. He continued to sleep with her at night, and he stopped riding on her back only when she became so frail that her legs buckled under her when he climbed aboard. There were times when I felt like shaking

Flint because of the way he treated Flo. If she stopped to rest, he pestered her until she agreed to groom him. If he was ready to move on before his now ancient mother, he would sometimes push her from behind, whimpering like an infant. And because of him she had to construct, each night, a larger nest than would have been necessary for herself alone.

But then I realized that without Flint, Flo would have had a very lonely old age. For as she became ever more frail, she spent less and less time with the other chimps. She needed Flint for company. If they came to a fork in the trail and she went one way and he another, it was just as likely that she would give in and follow him as vice versa. Even daughter Fifi, her close companion until this time, abandoned her mother now. For Fifi had given birth. She had to travel further afield to find enough food for herself and her infant.

One day we found Flo's body lying at the edge of one of the fast-flowing streams. Flint was sitting on the bank, gazing down at her. Every so often he clambered down and peered at her closely. Sometimes he pulled at her dead hand, as though begging her to wake and groom him. Then, disconsolate, he climbed up and sat, huddled and miserable, looking down at his lifeless mother. That night he climbed slowly into a nearby tree and into a nest that, a few nights before, he had shared with Flo.

I climbed the steep hillside until I could see him where he lay. As darkness fell he was still staring, his eyes wide open, towards that sad place in the stream.

Flint gradually became more and more depressed. At first he spent a few days with his brother Figan. But suddenly he left the group and raced back to where he had left his mother.

She was gone by then – the bushpigs make short work of dead animals so we had taken her body for burial. Flint did not search for her. He resumed his huddled posture, sitting near the stream where she had died. Nothing seemed to bring him out of his depression.

And by the time Fifi finally returned from a journey to the north, Flint had become sick. In his state of deep depression his immune system was probably so weakened that he had little resistance to infection.

Fifi did stay by him for a while. And he relaxed when she sat grooming him. But he lacked the strength, or the will, to follow when she moved on. And so, pausing many times to look back, she left him lying there. She never saw him again.

Flint died, three and a half weeks after losing his mother. I think the main cause of death was grief.

MADAM BEE AND HER DAUGHTER

Madam Bee was not as old as she looked. But for ten years she had
been afflicted by a paralyzed arm, the result of a polio epidemic that
had swept through Gombe. She had given birth to four offspring
but, probably because it had been so difficult for her to care for them
with only one good arm, the last two, born after the epidemic,
had died in infancy. Madam Bee's life had been a hard one.

Towards the end of her days, there was a very harsh dry season at Gombe. There was not much food and the chimpanzees had to walk long distances between one patch of fruit and the next. Madam Bee had just lost her last infant and these journeys exhausted her so that sometimes, when she finally reached her destination, she was too tired to climb.

This was hardly surprising, since she found it difficult to cope with tall trees at the best of times.

One day, after making such a long hot journey, Madam Bee lay stretched out on the ground and watched as her two daughters, adult Little Bee and adolescent Honey Bee, swung up to the high branches. With small calls of delight they began to feed on the ripe, juicy mabungo fruits. Only the old female's eyes indicated how much she longed to be up there too.

And then, after ten minutes, Little Bee started to collect fruits. They were large – tennis-ball sized – but she managed to carry three in her mouth with the stems between her teeth and two more in one hand. And then she climbed down and walked over to Madam Bee. She laid two of the fruits beside the old female and the two of them, mother and daughter, fed side by side, peaceful and content.

Little Bee was seen helping her mother on two other occasions.

GREMLIN AND GIMBLE

One day Gimble was following his mother, Melissa, through the long grass. Gremlin, his sister, brought up the rear. They were moving in single file, along one of the animal trails that wound its way across the top of an open ridge between two valleys. It was the end of the dry season, and the grass was as dry as straw.

Suddenly, as Melissa all but vanished where the trail led through an extra-tall patch of grass, Gremlin seized hold of her three-year-old brother and prevented him from following their mother. Gimble was bewildered and gave small cries of distress.

Gremlin struggled to gather him up, but he pulled away and tried to rush after Melissa, into the tall grass.

Quickly Gremlin pushed past her small brother and headed him off, shepherding him off the trail and insisting that he go around and not through that patch of long grass. Gimble's crying got louder, but soon the danger, whatever it might be, was safely passed and Gremlin allowed her brother to run after Melissa.

I went to look in the patch of tall grass. I moved cautiously, expecting to find a snake. At first I saw nothing – then suddenly I noticed that hundreds and hundreds of tiny ticks were clinging to the grass stems bordering the trail.

A whole brood must have just hatched.

Hastily I made the same detour that Gremlin had chosen for her brother. A while later Melissa stopped, and sitting in the shade, she began searching through her hair and picking off the many ticks that had dropped onto her as she passed by. They had already attached themselves, and probably their bites had begun to itch. Chimpanzees love to groom, as well as to be groomed, and Gremlin eagerly helped to detick her mother. But I didn't see her pick any off herself, and Gimble, thanks to his sister, was free as well.

I still marvel at that chance observation. It was remarkable that Gremlin noticed those minute ticks from her position behind Gimble. That she would then avoid that place herself was not surprising. But how wonderful that, because of her concern, she had also saved her brother from the irritating bites.

AUNTIE GIGI

We have already met Gigi, when she rescued young Freud from the just vengeance of an angry bushpig. Large, destined never to bear a child, she behaves, in many ways, more like a male than a female. But she has always been fascinated by infants and, over the years, she has acted as "Auntie" to one youngster after another, playing with and grooming them. And, when the mothers permitted, carrying them during travel.

But however good those relationships were, the child's mother always came first. Until, when Gigi was about thirty-eight years old, came the epidemic that claimed eight chimpanzee lives, including the mothers of Mel and Spindle. That was the beginning of a new phase in Gigi's life.

I have already told how Spindle adopted Mel and saved his life. After a year, though, that relationship gradually weakened. And then Spindle disappeared, never to return. We presume he died. It was then that Mel began to follow Gigi. She did not carry him or share her nest, as Spindle had. But she waited for him before moving off. And if other youngsters threatened Mel, they had Gigi to answer to. During that same epidemic Little Bee also died. By that time she had given birth herself, and she left a child, Dar Bee, who was almost the same age as Mel. At first Dar Bee divided her time between three individuals: her juvenile brother, a young adult male, and an adolescent female. None of them nurtured her as Spindle nurtured Mel, not even her own brother. They all tolerated her presence, but she was not carried, and she slept in her own small nest at night. But, being a tough youngster, she survived.

And then Dar Bee, too, attached herself to Gigi. It became common-place to see the large female wandering through the forests with the two infants trailing in her wake. Only when Gigi was sexually attractive so that the males gathered around her in large, excited groups, did the orphans separate themselves from their caretaker. Then we often found them on their own, two little babes in the wood.

During a recent visit to Gombe I encountered Gigi feeding on clusters of blossoms, golden yellow in the early-morning sunlight. Above us was the blue sky, and when I looked down the slope I could see the blue water of Lake Tanganyika shimmering through the trees. And feeding contentedly near Gigi were three orphans. For Mel and Dar Bee had been joined by Dharsi, a four-year-old male whose mother had died a few months before.

And so Gigi, although she has never had a baby of her own, was caring for three motherless youngsters, providing for each of them that sense of security that is so desperately important for the growing child – chimpanzee and human child alike. She has truly earned the honorary title we bestowed upon her long ago – Auntie Gigi.

UNDERSTANDING

One day, when I was following David Greybeard through the forest,
he stopped to rest beside one of the clear, fast-flowing streams.

I sat near him. It was very peaceful. The sun filtered down through
the canopy overhead, speckling the forest floor with golden flecks,
dancing on the racing, chattering water. There were secret rustles in
the undergrowth as small forest creatures went about their business
and birds flitted from branch to branch, searching for food.

I looked at David as he lay, gazing up at the greens and browns of
the forest ceiling. He glanced at me, then closed his eyes and slept.
As always I was moved by his trust. It has laid a great responsibility
on me, for I must never allow that trust to be betrayed. I lay down,
there beside him on the forest floor, at peace.

Some time later we roused ourselves. As David sat, looking around, perhaps wondering where to go, I spied a ripe red palm nut lying on the ground nearby. I picked it up and held it towards David, on my palm. He turned his head away. I moved my hand closer. Then David took the nut and, at the same time, closed his fingers around my hand. He glanced into my eyes, let go my hand, then dropped the nut to the ground.

It needed no scientific training to understand the message of reassurance conveyed by the gentle pressure of his fingers over mine – he rejected my gift but not the giving.

His message had no need of words – it was based on a far older form of communication and it bridged the centuries of evolution that divided us.

THE RESEARCH AT GOMBE

Since 1960 we have followed the life histories of more than 100 known chim-panzees. Initially I worked on my own, but subsequently I built up an inter-disciplinary team to help with the study.

Chimpanzees are so complex, and differences between individuals so pro-nounced, that we are still learning new things even after nearly forty years. Since 1975 Tanzanian field staff, recruited from villages surrounding the Gombe National Park, have played a key role in the research. Because they know and care about the chimpanzees and there is no danger of poaching, these chimpanzees whom we have come to know so well can live out their lives in safety.

THE PLIGHT OF CHIMPANZEES ACROSS AFRICA
AND THE WORLD

All across Africa chimpanzees are disappearing fast. This is not only due to the relentless destruction of their forest homes, but also because they are hunted – often for food. Even where they are not eaten, mothers are still shot so that their infants can be stolen, then sold. Some are sold overseas by unscrupulous dealers, for entertainment and for medical research. Some are bought as "pets" by local people, or as attractions in a bar or hotel. For every infant that is bought we estimate that up to ten chimpanzees have died in the forest. Conditions for chimpanzees in captivity are often grim. In Africa, those bought as pets may spend a few years living as a member of the family, but at adolescence, when they become so strong and potentially dangerous, they are banished to tiny cages or tied up on chains. In African zoos they are often starving (the keepers often cannot afford one meal a day for themselves). Even in the developed world many chimpanzees languish in small, dingy cages, sometimes alone. And in the laboratories they typically live in tiny, bare steel prisons – alone. The training of those used in entertainment is almost always harsh, often cruel. Many are dressed in stupid and inappropriate clothes that give people a completely wrong picture of chimpanzee nature.

It was to try to redress some of these wrongs, as well as to enable us to continue documenting the lives of the Gombe chimpanzees, that the Jane Goodall Institute was established.

THE JANE GOODALL INSTITUTE

Only if we understand can we care
Only if we care will we help
Only if we help shall all be saved

The Jane Goodall Institute was first established in the U.S.A. in 1977. Funds raised by the Institute enable us to continue gathering information about chimpanzees, at Gombe and elsewhere; to conduct conservation efforts; to help improve conditions for captive chimpanzees (and other animals) in zoos, medical research laboratories, and the entertainment trade. Today our work involves research, conservation, welfare, and education in Tanzania, Burundi, Congo, Uganda, Kenya, South Africa, and Ghana, as well as in the U.S.A., Taiwan, and Europe. One of our major efforts is to create sanctuaries for orphan chimpanzees whose mothers have been shot by hunters either for bushmeat or so that their infants can be stolen and sold.

Information about the Institute, how you can join and help us, can be obtained from any of our offices:

JGI (U.S.A.), P.O. Box 599, Ridgefield, Connecticut 06877
JGI (U.K.), 15 Clarendon Park, Lymington, Hampshire SO41 8AX
JGI (TZ), P.O. Box 727, Dar es Salaam, Tanzania
JGI (Congo), P.O. Box 1893, Pointe Noire, Congo
JGI (Canada), P.O. Box 477, Victoria Station, Westmount, QC, H3Z 2Y6
JGI (Germany/Austria/Switzerland), Herzogstrasse 60, D–80803 München
JGI (Taiwan ROC), 6F, No. 20 Sec. 2 Hsin–Sheng Sth. Rd, Taipei

ROOTS & SHOOTS

Roots creep underground everywhere and make a firm foundation. Shoots seem very weak, but to reach the light they can break open brick walls. Imagine the brick walls as all the problems humans have inflicted on our planet, from desertification to cruelty and war. Hundreds and thousands of roots and shoots, hundreds and thousands of young people around the world, can break through these walls. Together we can change the world.

Every individual matters
Every individual has a role to play
Every individual makes a difference

The members themselves decide what they can do, individually or as a group, to make the world a better place: by clearing up litter, saving energy, planting trees, caring for animals, and so on; by bringing extra smiles to people's faces, extra wags to the tails of dogs.

The first Roots & Shoots groups were born in Tanzania in February 1991. Today there are hundreds of groups in more than 38 countries; over 600 in North America alone. Through personal correspondence and newsletters members can be in contact with each other around the world. A primary goal, in each country, is to bring together members from different socio-economic and ethnic groups to work on joint projects.

For information on how to start a group, contact any of our offices.

Endpaper illustrations: Spindle and orphan Mel